M000159887

NOW
that

IS
AMAZING
GRACE

NOW *that*

IS
AMAZING
GRACE

William MacDonald

GOSPEL FOLIO PRESS
304 Killaly St. West Port Colborne, ON L3K 6A6
Available in the UK from JOHN RITCHIE LTD.
40 Beansburn, Kilmarnock, Scotland

NOW THAT IS AMAZING GRACE
Second edition Copyright © 2001
William MacDonald
All rights reserved

First edition published in 1995

Published by Gospel Folio Press
304 Killaly St. West
Port Colborne, ON   L3K 6A6

ISBN 1-882701-21-6

Cover design by J. B. Nicholson, Jr.

Printed in the United States of America

CONTENTS

Introduction . . . . *viii*

1. A Stupendous Problem 9
2. A Unique Solution 13
3. Now the Good News 19
4. God's Mind-boggling Grace 23
5. How to Appreciate Grace 29
6. A "Gospel" that is Bad News 45
7. How to Tell a Real Believer 55
8. Your Speech Betrays You 59
9. What's Wrong with Works? 63
10. Answer Me This Question 65
11. Grace Misused and Abused 71
12. How God Produces Holiness 75
13. It's Grace All the Way 83
14. Grace in Review 87

Endnotes 91

Grace is but glory begun,
and glory is but grace perfected.

—JONATHAN EDWARDS

INTRODUCTION

After a troubled childhood and youth, John Newton joined his father's ship in Mediterranean trade. He plunged to the depths of immorality, debauchery, and infidelity. Someone said that he could curse and swear for two hours without repeating himself. After being fired by his father, he served on slave ships, where he himself actually became a slave of his boss's African wife.

When he nearly perished in a violent storm at sea, he turned to the Lord, and later became a minister of the gospel which he had so despised.

His personal experience of salvation is enshrined in this much loved hymn. By a curious providence, the hymn has at times headed the hit charts in popular music circles among people who probably are strangers to the amazing grace of God.

Amazing grace! how sweet the sound,
That saved a wretch like me!
I once was lost, but now am found,
Was blind, but now I see!

'Twas grace that taught my heart to fear,
And grace my fears relieved:
How precious did that grace appear
The hour I first believed.

Through many dangers, toils, and snares,
I have already come;
'Tis grace hath brought me safe thus far,
And grace will lead me home.

When we've been there ten thousand years,
Bright shining as the sun,
We've no less days to sing God's praise
Than when we first begun.[1]

Chapter One

A STUPENDOUS PROBLEM

God had a problem. Well, not exactly. The great God is too powerful and wise to have problems. He only solves them. But it appears *to us* that He had a problem in figuring out a plan of salvation for mankind. We are simply using the language of human appearance when we say that He had a problem.

Now that we have cleared that up, what is the problem? Actually it arises from a seeming clash between two of the great attributes of God—His love and His righteousness.

On the one hand, God is a God of love. He loves people passionately. They are His crowning work. Among all the marvels of creation, He is delighted in a special way with humanity. He wants the companionship, the fellowship of every man, woman, boy, and girl for all eternity.

But the problem arises from the fact that we all are sinners and God is righteous. He can't look on sin with approval. He can't wink at sin, overlook it or condone it. Sin must be punished and the wages of sin is death. If sinners are ever going to be at home with God in heaven, their sins must somehow be put away. The penalty must be paid. People must be clean and pure to live with God.

So there you have the stupendous problem. On the one hand, God is love, and His love is not willing that any should perish. He doesn't desire the eternal destruction of anyone. He wants everyone to enjoy the splendors and delights of heaven forever. But God is also light. His righteousness demands that the sinner's sins must be atoned for. He demands full satisfaction for every evil thought, word, and deed. No unforgiven sinner can ever enter heaven.

Now how can God devise a plan of salvation that satisfies His love and yet does not compromise His righteousness? How can He be a just God and a Saviour at the same time? How can He be a righteous God and pardon ungodly sinners? That's the dilemma. The famous Greek philosopher, Socrates, once said to Plato, then his pupil, "It may be that God can forgive sins, but I don't see how."

Seven Requirements for Any Plan of Salvation

It was an act of indescribable grace when God decided to rescue fallen mankind. But once He made that decision, He had to devise a plan that would fully satisfy His love and His holiness. Since He loves everyone, His salvation must be:

• Offered to all. He doesn't want anyone left out.

• Sufficient for all. It must meet the needs of every person without exception.

• Something for which everyone is eligible. No amount of evil should be able to bar anyone from participation.

• Simple enough for anyone to understand. There's no use making an incomprehensible offer.

• Something which anyone can receive. The true religion must not have any conditions that some couldn't meet.

• There must be no possibility for human boasting. Pride is the parent sin, and there will be no pride in heaven. In order to exclude boasting, everyone must have the same fitness for heaven.

• Yet the plan must be one which God does not force on a person against his will.

11

The next chapter will present to us God's amazing solution to satisfy everyone of these requirements.

Chapter Two

A UNIQUE SOLUTION

There is only one conceivable solution to the divine dilemma. It lies in the word *substitution.* A suitable substitute must somehow be found to pay the penalty of the sins of the people. Most of us are familiar with the idea of substitution. In some athletic events, the coach sends someone onto the field as a substitute for another player. The average Hebrew believer in Old Testament times understood substitution. When he brought an animal to the altar of sacrifice and laid his hand on the animal's head, he pictured the transfer of his sins to a substitute that would die in his place.

Yes, the solution to the divine dilemma is to have a substitute die in the place of sinful humanity. But even here there are conditions to be met by the substitute.

The Substitute Must Pass Five Tests

• The substitute must be human. Otherwise the exchange would not be fair or equal.

• He must be a sinless person. Otherwise he would have to die for his own sins.

• He must be God. Only an infinite person could atone for the numberless sins of the human race. The value of the substitute must be great enough to cover all the sins of humanity—past, present, and future.

• He must shed his blood, because divine law has decreed that without the shedding of blood there is no forgiveness of sin. Life is in the blood and there must be life for life.

• He must be willing. Otherwise Satan could charge God with unjustly forcing an involuntary victim to die in the place of ungodly sinners.

Jesus Qualifies on All Counts

The only Person in the universe who meets these conditions is the Lord Jesus Christ.

• He became Man at Bethlehem. Born of the Virgin Mary, He is perfect Man.[1] As the great Christian hymn-writer, Charles Wesley, put it, "Our God contracted to a span, incomprehensibly made Man."

• He is God.[2] He has the attributes of God, the titles of God, and is equal with God the Father.

• He is without sin. The record cannot be denied. He knew no sin, He did no sin, and there is no sin in Him.[3]

• He shed His blood as a substitute for sinners on the cross of Calvary. Multitudes have availed themselves of the blood of Jesus Christ, God's Son, that cleanses from all sin.[4]

• He did it willingly so that sinners could be saved. There was no reluctance, no holding back. On the contrary, there was a joyful submission to the will of God.[5]

The truth of Christ as our substitute is found throughout the Bible. Isaiah boldly proclaimed,

Surely He has borne our griefs and carried our sorrows...He was wounded for our transgressions, He was bruised for our iniquities, the chastisement of our peace was upon Him, and by His stripes we are healed...and the Lord has laid upon Him the iniquity of us all.[6]

John the Baptist cried, *"Behold! The Lamb of God who*

takes away the sin of the world!"[7] Lost in wonder, the Apostle Paul said, *"The Son of God...loved me and gave Himself for me."*[8] Peter added his testimony: *"[He] Himself bore our sins in His own body on the tree."*[9] And not to be left out, John, the apostle of love, affirmed, *"He Himself is the propitiation for our sins, and not for ours only but also for the whole world."*[10]

God's Plan of Salvation Qualifies on All Counts

Since the Lord Jesus perfectly meets all the requirements for a substitutionary sacrifice, God can now proclaim His marvelous way of salvation, the good news of His grace. He can offer salvation as a gift to all who repent of their sins and receive His Son as Lord and Saviour by a definite act of faith.

• Notice that this salvation is available to all. The gospel says, *"Whoever believes on Him should not perish but have eternal life."*[11] If it depended on money, the poor would be left out.

• It is sufficient for all.[12] The death of this infinite Saviour has power to atone for all the sins of all the world. It is supremely adequate.

• Everyone is eligible for it because everyone is a sinner.[13] It's his very unfitness that qualifies anyone for God's salvation. It's a good thing that the gift of eternal life is not just for the intellectual, the wealthy, the good-looking, or the famous. Some of us would never qualify. Even if it were only for those who could read, walk, talk, or see, some would be excluded. Only the gospel suits the whole world.

• It is simple enough for anyone to understand. No one is too primitive or illiterate. In the gospel, the Lord Jesus says, *"Come."*[14] Nothing complicated about that. As William Cowper put it,

> *O! how unlike the complex works of man,*
> *Heaven's easy, artless, unencumbered plan!*

• Anyone can receive it.[15] Salvation is by repentance; anyone can do that. It is by faith; anyone can believe in the Lord Jesus Christ. No one is more credible than He, and nothing is more reasonable than for the creature to trust His Creator.

• Grace excludes boasting. It says, "I did all the sinning. Christ did all the saving. I claim His merits, and not my own. I have no right to enter heaven because of what I am or what I have done. Christ alone is my passport." If we could earn heaven by our performance or by our supposedly fine character, we could indulge in boasting. And there would be degrees of boasting, each one trying to outdo the other. Heaven would be a scene of constant one-upmanship, bickering, envy, jealousy, and rivalry. It wouldn't be heaven at all.

• Man is not coerced into accepting God's salvation.[16] The Creator made him a free moral agent. Strange as it may seem, not everyone *wants* to be saved. God does not force heaven on anyone. He will not take anyone to heaven against his or her will. You can be certain that any religion that grows by coercion, violence, and cruelty is not the true one.

So we see that God's way of salvation is perfect. It meets all the terms necessary to satisfy God's requirements and at the same time is available to all humanity. Christ's work on the cross enabled God to fully exercise His love without compromising His justice. The Psalmist says it poetically:

> *Mercy and truth have met together;*
> *Righteousness and peace have kissed each other.*[17]

Given the character of God and given the sinfulness of man, it is clear that it is the only possible way of salvation. People could never be saved in any other way.

Max Lucado points out:

No other world religion offers such a message. All others demand the rigid performance, the right sacrifice, the right chant, the right ritual, the right séance or experience. Theirs is a kingdom of trade-offs and barterdom. You do this, and God will give you that. The result? Either arrogance or fear. Arrogance if you think you've achieved it; fear if you think you haven't.

Christ's kingdom is just the opposite. It is a kingdom for the poor. A kingdom where membership is *granted,* not *purchased.* You are placed into God's kingdom. You are 'adopted.' And this occurs not when you do enough, but when you admit you *can't* do enough. You don't earn it; you simply accept it. As a result, you serve, not out of arrogance or fear, but out of gratitude.[18]

John MacArthur agrees that there are, after all, only two kinds of religion in all the world:

Every false religion ever devised by mankind or by Satan is a *religion of human merit.* Pagan religion, humanism, animism, and even false Christianity all fall into this category. They focus on what people must do to attain righteousness or please the deity.

Biblical Christianity alone is the *religion of divine accomplishment.* Other religions say, "Do this." Christianity says, "It is done" (cf. John 19:30). Other religions require that the devout person supply some kind of merit to atone for sin, appease deity, or otherwise attain the goal of acceptability. Scripture says Christ's merit is supplied on behalf of the believing sinner.[19]

Spurgeon asks:

Who would have thought of *the just Ruler dying for the unjust rebel?* This is no teaching of human mythology, or dream of poetic imagination. This method of expiation is only known among men because it is a fact. Fiction could not have devised it. God

19

Himself ordained it. It is not a matter which could have been imagined.[20]

Chapter Three

NOW THE GOOD NEWS

Perhaps the clearest verses in the Bible on the subject of salvation by grace apart from works are these:

Now to him who works, the wages are not counted as grace but as debt. But to him who does not work but believes on Him who justifies the ungodly, his faith is accounted for righteousness (Romans 4:4-5).

Notice the following truths in these verses:

When a person works and receives his pay, he is only receiving what the employer owes him. It is debt, not grace. That's not the way it is with God's salvation. Shocking as it may seem, God saves those who do *not* work, that is, who do not try to earn or deserve salvation but receive it as a free gift. It is only by ceasing to work that a person can enter God's rest.[1]

Another shocker is that it is only ungodly people whom He saves. Not good people, not people who do their best, but people who are willing to admit that they are *ungodly.* In other words, people who repent.

And pay attention to that word *"believe."* That is the crucial one. To believe means to receive Jesus Christ as Lord and Saviour. It means to accept Him as the One who paid the penalty of one's sins. It means to depend on Him as the only hope for heaven. The consistent testimony of Scripture is that salvation is by faith in Christ.[2]

When a person believes in Him, he is saved. And he can know it, not by his feelings, but by the infallible Word of God.

Come with Empty Hands

In order to be saved, a person must abandon any hope, not only of saving himself, but even of contributing to his or her own salvation. Several hymn writers state it well. Take Toplady's classic "Rock of Ages," for example:

> *Not the labors of my hands*
> *Can fulfill Thy law's demands;*
> *Could my zeal no respite know,*
> *Could my tears forever flow,*
> *All for sin could not atone;*
> *Thou must save, and Thou alone.*

Nothing in my hand I bring,
Simply to Thy cross I cling;
Naked, come to Thee for dress,
Helpless, look to Thee for grace;
Foul, I to the fountain fly,
Wash me, Saviour, or I die.

James Proctor reminds us that Christ finished the work for our redemption:

Weary, working, burdened one,
Wherefore toil you so?
Cease your doing; all was done
Long, long ago.

Till to Jesus' work you cling
By a simple faith,
"Doing" is a deadly thing,
"Doing" ends in death.

Cast your deadly "doing" down,
Down at Jesus' feet;
Stand in Him, in Him alone,
Gloriously complete.

"It is finished!" yes, indeed,
Finished every jot;
Sinner, this is all you need,
Tell me, is it not?

Chapter Four

GOD'S MIND-BOGGLING GRACE

Amazing grace! We sing about it, but do we know what it means?

First of all, what is grace? We can begin by saying that it is God's favor toward us. But it is more than that. It is His *undeserved* favor. Now let us go a step further. It is His undeserved favor to those who deserve the very opposite! It is His unfathomable ocean of kindness and generosity.

The words *grace* and *gift* are close relatives. Grace is a gift and for that reason it can neither be earned nor deserved. The minute you introduce any idea of debt or merit, you have eliminated grace. The gift of God's grace is of such enormous proportions that any thought of ever repaying it is completely ruled out. It is unspeakable and incomprehensible.

Now the true gospel is salvation by grace through faith alone.[1] Grace means you don't deserve it. Faith means you must receive it by a definite act of your will. No one understands the gospel unless he understands grace.

The grace of God is wonderful. It can take a repentant prostitute, forgive and cleanse her, make her a new woman, and destine her to be a companion of Jesus in eternal glory. It can take a dying thief, save him in the closing moments of his life, and escort him to paradise that very day.

Grace populates heaven with converted murderers, sex fiends, alcoholics, thieves, and liars. No sinner is beyond its saving power.

Grace has lifted millions out of a horrible pit and from the miry clay; set their feet on a rock, establishing their way; put a song in their heart, to glorify their God; and eventually has taken them to the many mansions in the Father's house.[2]

Oxford (and Cambridge) professor C. S. Lewis tells how the Lord overtook him when he was kicking and screaming, the most reluctant convert in all of England.

Then he adds,

> Who can duly adore that [grace] which will open the high gates to
> a prodigal who is brought in kicking, struggling, resentful, and
> darting his eyes in every direction for a chance of escape?[3]

Hymn writer Haldor Lillenas was right on key when he
wrote that the wonderful grace of Jesus is "broader than
the scope of our transgressions, greater far than all our
sin and shame."

Every true believer is often compelled to say, "I don't
know why the Lord ever showed grace to me. I certainly
am not worthy of such favor. The price He paid for me
was definitely too high."

Grace transcends reason and logic, but it doesn't
violate them. Reason would never have the shepherd die
for the sheep, the judge die for the condemned, or—most
incredible—the Creator die for the creature. Logic would
insist that the sinner die for his sins, that the penalty of
the broken law be carried out. Grace does the unthink-
able.

Someone has described the marvel of grace this way:

> Grace is not looking for good people whom it may approve, for it
> is not grace but justice to approve goodness; but it is looking for
> condemned, guilty, speechless, and helpless people whom it may
> save, sanctify, and glorify.

Grace is Better than Mercy

When a condemned criminal receives a reduced sentence, we say that the judge has shown him mercy. Imprisonment rather than the death sentence would be an act of mercy. The guilty doesn't get the retribution he deserves.

Grace is better than that. It acquits the guilty sinner. It imputes righteousness to him. It silences the law's condemning voice.

Grace is Better than Justice

Grace and justice are completely opposite. A man is asking for justice when he says, "I am a good person and I want what I deserve." Hell is what he deserves. Don't ever ask God for justice!

Grace says, "I am guilty, but I believe Christ died to pay the penalty for my sins, and I receive Him as Lord and Saviour. I don't deserve eternal life but I receive it as a free gift from God."

Jesus gave a parable that illustrates the difference between justice and grace.[4] There was a farmer who needed workers for his vineyard. Early in the morning, some men offered to work all day for a denarius, a silver coin. They made a definite contract with him for that amount.

During the day, he hired others who agreed to work for whatever he was inclined to pay them.

At the end of the day, the first workers got their denarius. All the others received the same amount—but it was much more *per hour*. The first men got justice. The others got grace. Grace is better than justice.

Grace is a Better Principle than Law

The law tells a person what he must do in order to attain a righteous standing. Grace gives him a righteous standing before God, then tells him to walk worthy of it.

The law says, "Do and you will live." Grace says, "Live and you will do."

The law says, "Try and obey." The language of grace is, "Trust and obey."

Law tells you what to do, but does not give you the power to do it, and curses you if you don't. Grace teaches you what to do, gives you the power to do it, and rewards you when you do. So law carries the threat of punishment while grace carries the promise of reward.

Law condemns the best, since even the best cannot keep the Ten Commandments. Grace justifies the worst. Law reveals sin. Grace takes away sin. Law encourages boasting. Grace excludes boasting.

29

Law says, "You must…You shall…You shall not." Grace says, "You should…You ought."[5] One tells what I have to do; the other tells what my new nature wants to do.

Under law, the work is never finished. Grace tells of the One who finished the work. The law demands, "You shall love…" Grace announces, "God so loved…" The law lays heavy burdens on people. The burdens of grace are light. Law is a system of bondage, grace of liberty. It is the difference between pressure and privilege.

There is no mercy in the law. It is cold, hard, and inflexible. Grace tells of a God who is rich in mercy.

Chapter Five

HOW TO APPRECIATE GRACE

No one will ever appreciate grace until he or she recognizes four great facts: who Jesus is; what He did; for whom He did it; and what it means for the recipient.

Who Jesus Is

He is not a mere human like ourselves, but rather:

• The Mighty God who filled the universe with untold wonders.

• The Creator who designed the thousands of parts of our bodies and put wisdom in our minds. By Him all things exist and consist.

•The Sovereign who has all power, all knowledge, and who is present everywhere at the same time.

• The Holy One to whom sin is utterly foreign.

• The One who was rich in glory, majesty, honor, everything desirable from all eternity. Angels veil their faces in His presence. He holds the waters in the palm of His hand, measures earth with a span, and calculates the dust of the earth in a measure. He weighs the mountains in scales, and the hills in a balance.[1] We do not deserve that such a Person should be interested in us.

What He Did

He loved us without cause and with perfect knowledge of everything we would ever do and be.

He left the glories of heaven, where He was the Object of the worship of myriads of holy angels, to be born in the stench of a cattle-shed. "Lo! within a manger lies He who built the starry skies."

Coming down into the muck and mire of the human race, He endured all kinds of abuse from His creatures. Imagine God's Son allowing men to cover His face with their filthy spit. Think of Him becoming the song of the drunkards.

He suffered as no one has ever suffered. He was wounded, bruised, and pierced. He was beaten until His back was like a plowed field, and His facial features were no longer recognizable. His tormentors pulled the hair out of His cheeks. All His bones were yanked out of joint. As Graham Kendrick wrote, "Hands that flung the stars into space, to cruel nails surrendered."

All of this was *nothing* compared to what it meant to the Son of God to be forsaken by God, His Father. When He prayed, it was as if the heavens were dead. In a way we will probably never understand, God placed the debt of our sins on His lovely Son, and then poured out the torrent of His judgment until the Lord Jesus paid the debt in full.

He died as a substitute, paying the penalty of sins that others committed and expecting nothing in return. It was on the old rugged cross "where the dearest and best for a world of lost sinners was slain."

> *Wonders of wonders! Vast surprise!*
> *Could bigger wonder be,*
> *That He who built the starry skies*
> *Once bled and died for me?*
>
> *Amazing, startling sacrifice,*
> *Confounding all our thought!*
> *Stupendous, staggering purchase price*
> *Which our redemption bought!*   (Author unknown)

J. Oswald Sanders wrote,

The most astute intellects of all time have delved into the inner meaning of Christ's death on the cross, but all have failed to plumb its infinite depths. Like Paul, they have withdrawn with the cry of bafflement: *'O the depth of the riches both of the wisdom and knowledge of God! How unsearchable are His judgments, and His ways past finding out'* (Rom 11:33).

Harold St. John said that the grace of God, as seen in the cross of Christ, never means a thing to us until it takes our breath away and becomes the greatest thing in life.

Spurgeon calls on us to behold the wonder of it:

Jesus has borne the death penalty on our behalf…There He hangs upon the cross! This is the greatest sight you will ever see: Son of God and Son of man! There He hangs, bearing pains unutterable—the Just for the unjust, that He might bring us to God.

Oh, the glory of that sight! The innocent suffering! The Holy One condemned! The Ever-blessed made a curse! The Infinitely Glorious put to a shameful death![2]

The Saviour did not deserve the vile treatment He received. We are not worth the stupendous price He paid. It was too much. If we could fully take it in, we would "…dissolve our hearts in thankfulness and melt our eyes to tears."

Of course, His death was not the end of the story. He rose from the dead three days later. If He had not risen, His death would have been no different from any other person's. But it *was* different. He was the first to rise from the dead to die no more. He was the first to rise in a glorified body. His resurrection demonstrated Him to be the Son of God with power. It was proof that God was absolutely satisfied with His work on the cross. And it is the pledge that all who believe on Him will rise from the dead in a glorified body, just like His resurrection body.

For Whom He Did It

We were ungodly sinners, ungrateful wretches, undeserving worms. We were lost, helpless, and hopeless. We richly deserved hell. There was nothing lovable about us. We didn't want to have anything to do with the Lord. We didn't want any celestial Big Brother running our lives.

At our best, our righteousness was like filthy rags. At our worst, we were capable of murdering our God. The prophet was right when he said that the heart of man is deceitful and desperately wicked above all things.[3] No one can know the depths of its depravity.

Here we must pause and distinguish between the way we see ourselves and the way God sees us. Many people have kind, amiable dispositions. They are good neighbors and attend church regularly. They reach out to the poor, ill, and disabled. You know people like that and you may be one of them—a decent, law-abiding citizen, friendly and outwardly respectable.

But we must never forget that God's standard is perfection, and all of us have fallen short of that standard.[4] There is not one of us who does not sin. None of us would want our thought life to be made public. Even if we have not broken all ten of the commandments, we are capable of doing it. What we *are* is a lot worse than anything we have ever *done.* Some may be better than others, but God sees us all as desperate sinners in perilous and urgent need of salvation.

We were dead in trespasses and sins. We walked according to the course of this world, led around by the devil. We were children of disobedience, living to fulfill the desires of the flesh and of the mind. By nature we were children of wrath, without Christ, without God, and without hope.[5]

We are the kind of people for whom Christ died. What makes it all the more remarkable is that we are so insignificant. We are scarcely visible when viewed from an altitude of 10,000 feet. How much more infinitesimal we appear when seen from billions of light years away. And yet He loved us!

Vernon C. Grounds agrees:

Considering the utter insignificance of our earth, it is hard to believe that the Creator of the cosmos cares about what happens to the human family that has been cynically described as a semi-invisible rash on the skin of a sub-microscopic planet in a second rate solar system.

And then Grounds add, "The astonishing truth is that God does care.[6]

No one can appreciate the grace of Christ until he comes to the cross and says, in the words of D. T. Niles, "I did that to Him and He did that for me."[7]

What It Means For the Believer

Grace could have done *less* for believers than it actually did. For instance, it could have given unending life on earth without the infirmities of aging. That, in itself, would have been wonderful. It could have saved men and women from the everlasting burnings—even more wonderful!

But God was not satisfied with some halfway measure. Having given His best in the sacrifice of His Son, He decided not to withhold the richest inheritance His mind could conceive. Here are some of the built-in benefits of the gospel of grace:

Joy. This is supernatural delight that is totally independent of circumstances. Its opposite is not sin but sorrow. It arises from this relationship to God and to the Lord

Jesus. Therefore it is as steadfast as that relationship.

Peace. Those who are justified by faith enjoy peace with God. Their conflict with the Almighty ended when they flew the flag of surrender. Then there follows an other-worldly serenity, calmness, and poise from knowing that the Lord is in control.

Hope. In the New Testament, hope usually refers to the believer's future in heaven. Unlike the meaning of the word in common usage, this hope does not contain the slightest particle of doubt because it is based on the certain promise of God. The believer is as sure of heaven as if he were already there.

Rest. When Jesus said, *"Come to Me...and I will give you rest,"* He was referring to salvation rest. It is the rest that comes when a person stops trying to work for eternal life, and when he rests on the finished work of Christ. But Jesus also spoke of another rest: *"Take My yoke upon you and learn from Me...and you will find rest for your souls."* This is the rest found in serving the Lord and in following His example of gentleness and lowliness of heart.

Freedom. The truth makes people free—not free to indulge the passions of the flesh, but free to live righteously, to please God, and to serve Him. The Christian is freed from the dominion of sin and the bondage of the law, but he is not lawless. Rather, he is bound by love to Christ.

Purpose in life. Not until a person is born again does he find the real reason for his existence. Only then does life become meaningful. At last, he finds something (or, better, Someone) to live for and Someone to die for. At last he finds fulfillment in total commitment to the Son of God. He now has a philosophy of life that answers the age-old questions about creation, about the presence of evil, and about the fact of death. He has come home.

Satisfaction. The believer is never satisfied with himself or with his attainments, but he is satisfied with Christ. As D. Martyn Lloyd-Jones said, "There is nothing that my heart can crave for but He can more than satisfy."[8]

Grace provides all this, but much, much more. The moment sinners receive the Lord by faith, they are:

• Recipients of eternal life.[9] This priceless gift is the very life of Christ, the more abundant life which the Saviour promised.[10] Even the unsaved have endless *existence,* but only believers have Christ within them, the hope of glory.[11] Natural life is received by birth and is subject to death. Eternal life comes by the new birth and is deathless. Eternal life is nothing less than union with God. Astounding!

• Forgiven.[12] By a miracle of grace, God forgives and removes sins as far as the East is from the West, never to remember them again. All the charges against the penitent were nailed to the Cross.[13] They are gone. That is why Samuel W. Gandy could write:

> *I hear the accuser roar*
> *Of ills that I have done;*
> *I know them well, and thousands more;*
> *Jehovah findeth none.*

• Redeemed.[14] This means that at the staggering cost of Christ's precious blood, people are bought back from the slave market of sin. No purchase was ever more costly, no transaction more mind-boggling. What a wonderful exchange! Never have so many owed so much to One Person!

• Saved.[15] Not only are believers delivered from everlasting punishment in hell, they are saved from the present evil world system and preserved for God's heavenly kingdom. They were saved from the *penalty* of sin when they first believed. They are being saved from its *power* by Christ's present ministry. They will be saved from its very *presence* when they reach their eternal home.

• Accepted in the Beloved.[16] God now sees His trusting child in Christ, and accepts him or her on that basis. Anyone who is in Christ stands before God in all the acceptability of His beloved Son. In the Person of the Lord Jesus, he is as near to the Father as Jesus is. It is not who he is that counts, but his union with Christ; not a person's performance, but Christ's Person and work.

• Complete in Christ.[17] Even though it stretches the edges of belief, it is absolutely true: the one who trusts the Saviour is absolutely fit for heaven. The reason is that Christ is his fitness. If a person has Christ, he requires nothing more as far as eligibility for the Father's house. The believer stands in Jesus' merits, not in his own. On a scale of 1 to 10, he is 10.

• Loved as Christ is loved.[18] Not only is the true Christian as near to God as Christ is; he is also as dear to God. The Father loves him with the same love with which He loves His Son. Therefore, we are not exaggerating to say that God cannot love His own people any more than He already does. *This awesome truth deserves to be better known, believed, and enjoyed!*

• Justified.[19] When an unrepentant sinner stands before God as his Judge, there can be only one verdict— Guilty! But when a repentant believer is in the dock, the picture changes. God is still the Judge but the Lord Jesus is the Defense Attorney. When the charges are read, Christ steps forward and says, in effect, "Your Honor, My client is guilty." Then, pointing to the wounds in His own hands, feet, and side, He continues: "But I paid the penalty of his crimes on the cross of Calvary. I plead the merits of My substitutionary work on his behalf."

The Judge nods in satisfaction. "The accused is acquitted," He says. "I reckon him to be righteous. I cannot find

41

a single sin for which to condemn him to hell. Case dismissed!"

It was this heart-warming truth that gave W. Noel Tomkins the boldness to hurl out the challenge:

> *Reach my blest Saviour first;*
> *Take Him from God's esteem;*
> *Prove Jesus bears one spot of sin;*
> *Then tell me I'm unclean!*

Roy Hession told of an Englishman who went to France on his holiday, driving his Rolls Royce. Unfortunately he must have been on a rough road one day, and his rear axle broke. The local garages were unable to replace the axle, but a call to the manufacturer in England brought a new one, together with two mechanics to install it. Months later when no bill had come, the Englishman wrote to Rolls Royce, recounted the incident, and asked for an invoice. The company replied, "We have searched our files carefully and can find no record of a Rolls Royce ever having a broken axle." That's something like the way it is with the believer in Christ. God can search His records carefully and can find no record of sin on that believer, as far as guilt and penalty are concerned.

• Sanctified.[20] Sanctification is a doctrinal marvel, describing the fact that God sets believers apart from sin and the world to belong to Himself. As soon as they are saved, they are sanctified positionally. Then they are taught to live in holiness, consistent with their position. However, only in heaven will the work be completed.

• Served by Christ.[21] As Great High Priest, Intercessor, Advocate, and Helper, He gives grace, consolation, and encouragement. He intercedes for His own. When they sin, He goes to work to restore them to communion. Day and night He pleads the cause of His people against the accusations of Satan.

• Indwelt.[22] The Third Person of the Holy Trinity enters the body of the child of God at the moment of his new birth. It is amazing but true that that frail human body is henceforth the temple of the Holy Spirit. The Spirit is the power for holiness, worship, and service. He is responsible for the startling change that characterizes the life of a saint.

• Baptized by the Spirit.[23] This ministry of the Spirit makes those who repent and believe on Christ members of His body. At the moment of salvation, the believer receives the extraordinary privilege of becoming a member of the greatest fellowship on earth, the Church. This new society has Christ as its Head and all true Christians as members. No words can describe the close bond that unites Christ's followers to Him and to one another.

• Sealed.[24] In addition to the preceding ministries of the Spirit, He is also given as a seal, signifying ownership and a guarantee of eternal preservation. Every blood-bought saint has this seal.

• Given the Earnest.[25] Just as sure as a believer has the Holy Spirit, he is certain of the entire inheritance, including the glorified body in heaven. The earnest is a down payment or a pledge. An engagement ring is sometimes used to illustrate the earnest of the Spirit.

• Anointed.[26] When a person is saved, he receives the Holy Spirit as an anointing. This includes two important ministries. First, there is the teaching ministry of the Spirit, enabling the convert to distinguish between truth and error. Second, he is singled out for service, just as prophets, priests, and kings were anointed in the Old Testament.

• Access to God in prayer.[27] What a breathtaking wonder—that the least one in the kingdom of God has instant and constant access to the Sovereign of the universe! By faith he moves from earth to the Throne Room in heaven, the Most Holy Place, and has audience with the King of kings and Lord of lords. This privilege did not come cheaply; it was purchased by the blood of the Lord Jesus.[28]

To help make the Christian's prayer life more vivid, Bernard of Clairvaux suggested centuries ago: "Thus pray, as if taken up and presented before His face on the Highest Throne, where thousands of thousands are serving Him."

• New citizenship.[29] Conversion involves a change of citizenship—from earthly to heavenly. People who were once earth dwellers become aliens, pilgrims, and strangers here. They recognize a new Ruler and obey higher laws, but at the same time they respect human authority and obey local laws, as long as these don't conflict with the higher ones. Their "old country" is doomed to destruction; their new country is eternal.

• Children of God.[30] Salvation also involves a change of parentage. The birth certificate of the redeemed lists God as Father. Think of it—not the child of a president or king, but of the Creator and Sustainer of the universe. No honor could be higher!

• Sons of God.[31] Whether male or female, believers are brought into the divine family as adults, with all the privileges and responsibilities of adults. They are not treated like children with legalistic bondage but with the liberty of freeborn sons and daughters.

• Heirs of God and co-heirs with Jesus Christ.[32] The titles are self-explanatory, and yet their depth eludes us. Who could ever measure the wealth of God the Father and of His Son? The totals would be astronomical. Yet they are the measure of the inheritance that

45

belongs to everyone who loves the Lord.

• Holy and royal priests.[33] The Old Testament priesthood was confined to one tribe, one family. But now all believers are priests. Their function is twofold. First, to offer to God their love, their lives, their praise, their possessions, and their service. Then, they are appointed to show forth the excellencies of the One who called them out of darkness into His marvelous light.

• More than conquerors.[34] How can anyone be more than a conqueror? He either wins or he doesn't. How can he do more than win? The thought here is that believers are already victorious, even when they are in the thick of the battle. The outcome is certain. They are on the winning side. At any particular time, the waves may seem to be against them, but the tide is sure to win.

• Destined to be conformed to His image.[35] To be with Him, His spotless bride, for all eternity. J. N. Darby called this a "thought beyond all thought"—to be transformed into the moral and spiritual image of the Lord. Lost in wonder, he asked:

And is it so—I shall be like Thy Son?
Is this the grace that He for me has won?
Father of glory, (thought beyond all thought!)
In glory to His own blest likeness brought!

• In short, blessed with all spiritual blessings in

Christ.[36] As one of God's friends said, "Here let us pause, and worship. I at least must do so; for my soul's eyes ache, as though I had been gazing at the sun."[37] And, to borrow the words of one of Jane Austen's characters, believers have to learn to tolerate being happier than they deserve.[38]

Grace to the Max

Actually, the believer in Christ is better off than he ever would have been if sin had never entered. To put it another way, he is better off in Christ than he ever would have been in an unfallen Adam. The couplet is true:

> *In Christ the sons of Adam boast*
> *More blessings than their father lost.*

In his original innocence, Adam would never have been accepted in the Beloved or complete in Christ. He would never have been a son of God. He would not have had the hope of a home in heaven, or of being conformed to the image of Christ. He would never have enjoyed the blessings listed above.

As long as he didn't sin, he was assured of continued life on earth. But he would not have had the life of Christ. He would not have been permanently indwelt by the Holy Spirit. He would never have enjoyed the privileges that belong to a sinner saved by grace.

47

And there was always the awful possibility that he would fall into sin and thus be condemned. The threat of death hung over Adam and Eve like the sword of Damocles. As we know, Adam did sin, and his sin brought an avalanche of sorrow, suffering, and death. But God sent His Son to provide the way of salvation, and to enrich believers beyond human calculation. So pardoned sinners are better off than if they had never sinned. *"...Sin abounded, [but] grace abounded much more."*[39]

God's favor is grace from beginning to end, awesome, breathtaking, fathomless, abounding, greater than all our sin. As someone has said, every moment spent out of hell is by the grace of God.

Chapter Six

A "GOSPEL" THAT IS BAD NEWS

There is another kind of gospel, a *false* gospel. It is not good news at all, and yet it is the message that most people in the world believe. It says that good people go to heaven. It says that you earn your salvation by good works or deserve it by good character. Most religions of the world teach this doctrine in one form or another. It seems right to people, but the Bible says it ends in death, that is, eternal separation from God.[1]

It is not new. In fact, it goes all the way back to the Garden of Eden. Adam and Eve tried to cover their sinful nakedness with coverings of fig leaves. They wanted to make themselves fit for God's presence through something that they could do. But God had to show them it was all a big mistake. So He clothed them with the hides of animals. To do this, the animals had to die. Their blood had to be shed. All Adam and Eve had to do was accept God's provision by faith. God was teaching them that sin separates from God, that man cannot bridge the gap, and that sinners can approach God only on the basis of a substitutionary sacrifice whose blood has been shed.

Cain should have learned from his parents' mistake. Instead, he brought a bloodless offering to God, the result of his own labor—a flat rejection of God's way and a willful rejection of God's Word. It resulted in eternal damnation. The false gospel *seems* right, but it leads to death.

Yet after all these centuries, it is still the religion of choice. When his #2 legal aide died, a president of the United States said, "My deepest hope is that…[his] soul will receive the grace and salvation that his good life and good works earned."

A noted pastor, famed for his emphasis on the power of positive thinking, said, "Just so we think good thoughts and just so we do good, we believe all will go to heaven."

A faithful preacher may lecture for forty minutes on the fact that salvation is by grace through faith and not by works. At the end of the message, he stands at the door and asks a visitor, "Are you saved?"

The visitor replies, "I'm doing my best."

A Christian asked an acquaintance, "Are you saved?"

The acquaintance answered, "How can anyone know?" He realized that if salvation is by character or deeds, no one can be sure that he qualifies. The goal is too indefinite and elusive.

Salvation by works is so deeply ingrained in the human mind that it takes a supernatural work of the Spirit of God to eradicate it. People want to believe that they can save themselves or at least contribute to their salvation. It caters to their pride. They don't like to think of themselves as the objects of grace, or, as they say, "charity." It is offensive for them to think that they can't earn heaven.

And so they cling tenaciously to salvation by good works or good character. Even after many people are truly saved by grace, they lapse back into the idea that they must work in order to keep themselves saved. The church today is leavened with this heresy.

Words that are close relatives of this false gospel are law-keeping, works, and debt. In other words, salvation is a debt that God owes to the sinner because of his law-keeping or meritorious works.

The idea is that God, the Judge, holds a set of scales. He puts a person's good works on one side, and his bad works on the other. The side that is heavier determines his destiny—heaven or hell. Of course, he can't know until he dies which way the scales will tip.

That is not grace. Grace and works are completely opposite. The minute you try to mix them, it is no longer grace.[2] For instance, it is not grace to say that we are saved by living a Christian life. It is not grace to say that we are saved by any kind of works. Nor is it grace to say that we are saved by faith *plus* works.

Grace declares we are saved by faith plus *nothing*.

The Rich but Sad Young Ruler

Once there was a rich young ruler who believed in salvation by works.[3] He came to Jesus and asked, *"What good thing shall I do that I might have eternal life?"* He wanted to earn his salvation.

When Jesus quoted six of the Ten Commandments to show him the impossibility of gaining heaven by works, the young man pridefully boasted that he had kept all those commandments. But he really hadn't. He had not loved his neighbor as himself. If he had, he would have shared his wealth with the poor. Covetousness was his besetting sin. By breaking one of the commandments, he had broken all ten, because they are a chain of ten links. He needed to be saved by grace, not by works.

Counterfeit Tickets to Heaven

The most deep-seated heresy in the human mind is that salvation is by works; that good people go to heaven. Here is a sample of works that people depend on as a ticket to heaven:

• **Religious observances:**

Baptism. It should be understood that this rite is for those who are already saved. It is a public confession of Christ, and an identification with Him in His death, burial, and resurrection.

Confirmation. A church tradition, it is not ever found anywhere in the Bible and therefore could scarcely be a means of salvation.

Confession. Sins cannot be forgiven by confession to a man. What God is waiting to hear is confession of Jesus Christ as Lord and Saviour.

Holy communion. Like baptism, this is for those who are decided Christians. It is a remembrance of the Lord in His death.

Penance. This refers to any activity in which a person

engages in an attempt to atone for his sins. The word is not found in the New Testament. God wants sinners to repent, that is, to acknowledge their sin and turn to Him for forgiveness.

Regular attendance at church services and *church membership.* While admirable, church attendance has no saving value. The only membership that counts with the Lord is membership in the true Church, the body of Christ, made up of all true believers. It is not a *means* of salvation but a *result* of faith in Christ.

Tithing. For an unbeliever to give a certain percent of his income to a church is useless as far as gaining merit with God. Frankly, God does not want his money. He wants to see his repentance and faith.

Fasting. Self-denial may be good for a person's health, and, for Christians, it may help in spiritual concentration. But for unbelievers, it is invalid as a way to please God.

Prayers. The prayer God is waiting to hear from an unsaved person is, "God, be merciful to me, the sinner, and save me for Jesus' sake."

Extreme Unction. In this sacrament, a priest prays for the recovery and salvation of a person who is in critical condition. It is without scriptural authority and guarantees neither life on earth or eternal life.

• Law-keeping

The Ten Commandments. As we will see later, the purpose of these laws is to reveal sin and not to wash it away.

The Golden Rule. It is an ideal policy to do unto others as you would have them do unto you. But to obey it perfectly is beyond human power.

Any other set of rules. The New Testament is emphatic in teaching that a person can do nothing meritorious to save himself.

• Good character

Leading a good life. No matter how good our life is, it falls short of God's standard, which is His Son. One sin makes a sinner, and the wages of sin is death.

Being better than others. Almost anyone can say he is better than someone else. There is always somebody lower on the totem pole. Sorry, this boast will not do. If it were sufficient, then everyone would be saved except the worst sinner who ever lived.

• Good works

Gifts to charity. Compassion requires that we share with others who are in need. To speak against gifts to charity would be like speaking against motherhood. But the point is: these cannot atone for sins.

Doing one's best. Everyone should do that, but good works are not the savior. Jesus is.

• Heredity and family

Being born of godly parents. Salvation is not a matter of heredity. It does not run in the blood. Rather, each individual must make a personal response to the gospel.

Having a minister, priest, or rabbi in the family. No one becomes a believer through someone else's vocation. We are not saved by our human associations.

Having been a good father or mother, or having raised a good family. This is commendable, but it is not enough. We are not saved by anything good that we can do.

Not one of these—or any combination of them—can save a person. If they could, then Christ didn't need to die. The reason He died, was buried, and rose again, was because there is no other way of salvation than by faith in Him.

If you look over the list, you will see that not one item is within the reach of everyone in the world. In fact, you cannot think of any so-called good work that can be performed by everyone without exception. When you think of people who have neither arms nor legs, or those who are blind or penniless or one minute away from death, you will realize that salvation by works is a poor gospel. There is no good news in it.

For centuries, people have tried to win heaven by every strategy that the human mind could devise: meditation, self-denial, austerity, physical torture (such as climbing stairs on their knees), pilgrimages, monasticism, or payment of money. It is an exercise in futility. Nothing but the blood of Christ can wash away the stains of sin.

The Jesus-plus Fallacy

There are many who admit that faith in Christ is necessary, but they quickly add some other requirement. In the early days of the church, some taught that circumcision was also necessary. Today people add baptism, speaking in tongues, keeping the Sabbath, law keeping, and similar works. It is absolutely false. The Lord Jesus Christ is the sole and sufficient Saviour. He will not share the honor of Saviourhood with anyone or anything else. Salvation is by grace through faith plus nothing. Grace is His part; faith is ours.

The False Gospel Exposed

The false gospel is fatally flawed. The Bible repeatedly says that no one can ever be saved by law-keeping or by good works.[4] These things cannot atone for sins.

On the other hand, there are many verses in the Bible that say that salvation is by faith in Christ, entirely apart from works.[5]

A person seeking salvation by his works can never know that he is saved. He never knows if he has done enough good works or the right kind. But when you are saved by grace through faith, you can *know* you are saved on the authority of the Word of God. You know when you have received a gift. That is what the Bible means when it says, *"Therefore it is of faith that it might be according to grace, that it might be sure...."*[6]

A person under law can never be eternally secure because he doesn't know what he might do in the future. The fatal flaw of the works gospel is that everything depends on self.

The gospel of grace guarantees that no sheep of Christ will ever perish. John Kent's hymn reflects this confidence:

> *What from Christ the soul can sever,*
> *Bound by everlasting bands?*
> *Once in Him, in Him forever,*
> *Thus the eternal covenant stands:*
> *None shall pluck thee*
> *From the Saviour's mighty hands.*

People trying to work for or earn their salvation are slaves, endlessly striving but never achieving. Jesus promised believers that when He made them free, they would be free indeed.

The key word of the false gospel is *Do*. The key word of grace is *Done*. Christ has already finished the work of redemption. So you don't have to.

By nature, people don't like grace. They don't want it for themselves and they don't want God to show it to others. In this respect, they are something like a dog in a manger. It doesn't eat hay, and drives any other animal away. The religious leaders of Jesus' day shut up the kingdom of God against people. They didn't enter themselves and tried to prevent others from doing so.

It was so with the legal experts. They withheld God's Word from the people, did not go in themselves, and hindered those who were trying to enter.

Law persecutes grace. In Old Testament times, Ishmael mocked Isaac. Paul saw in the incident an illustration of this fact.[7] And it is seen even more starkly in the crucifixion of Christ. It was the legalists who engineered the death of Him who brought grace and truth.

Chapter Seven

HOW TO TELL A REAL BELIEVER

You can tell which of these platforms—law or grace—a person is standing on when you ask these simple questions: "Are you saved?" or "Are you a Christian?"

A true believer will say something like this: "Yes, I am saved, but it is only by the grace of God, not by anything that I have done."

There are some notable examples in the Bible of people who had a good appreciation of grace. Ruth, for example, was a member of a despised and doomed minority. When a man named Boaz showed unusual and unexpected kindness to her, she said, "Why have I found favor in your eyes, that you should take notice of me, since I am a foreigner?"[1] She understood grace.

After the Lord had made an unconditional covenant with David, the latter said, *"Who am I, O Lord God? And what is my house, that You have brought me this far?"*[2] David knew he was undeserving.

When David practically adopted the handicapped son of Jonathan, the latter asked, *"What is your servant, that you should look upon such a dead dog as I?"*[3] Mephibosheth realized that the king could have had him killed, because he, Mephibosheth, was the grandson of Saul, who had been relentless in his murderous pursuit of David.

Paul never got over the fact that he, a former persecutor of the Church, should be called to be an apostle:

> *To me, who am less than the least of all the saints, this grace was given, that I should preach among the Gentiles the unsearchable riches of Christ, and to make all men see what is the fellowship of the mystery...*[4]

He gladly admitted that he was unworthy of such a calling.

Hymns that Say It Well

Many Christian hymns eloquently express a grateful recognition of the grace that God has shown to those who believe. The best known, perhaps, is John Newton's immortal verse:

> *Amazing grace! how sweet the sound,*
> *That saved a wretch like me!*
> *I once was lost but now am found,*
> *Was blind, but now I see.*

(It is a mystery how many people love this hymn and even sing it, yet they still believe they are saved by their good life!)

Along the same line are the words of Isaac Watts:

> *Alas! and did my Saviour bleed?*
> *And did my Sov'reign die?*
> *Would He devote that sacred head*
> *For such a worm as I?*

Charles Gabriel recognized that his salvation was all of grace:

> *I stand all amazed at the love Jesus offers me,*
> *Confused at the grace that so freely He proffers me;*
> *I tremble to know that for me He was crucified,*
> *That for me, a sinner, He suffered, He bled, and died.*

Here is a conversation that actually took place when Charles Simeon first met John Wesley:[5]

SIMEON: I understand that you are called an Arminian[6]; and I have been sometimes called a Calvinist, and therefore I suppose we are to draw daggers. But before I consent to begin the combat, I will ask you a few questions. Do you feel yourself a depraved creature, so depraved that you would never have thought of turning to God if God had not first put it into your heart?

WESLEY: Yes, I do indeed.

SIMEON: And do you utterly despair of commending yourself to God by anything you can do; and look to salvation solely through the blood and righteousness of Christ?

WESLEY: Yes, solely through Christ.

SIMEON: But suppose that you were first saved by Christ, are you not somehow or other to save yourself afterwards by your own power?

WESLEY: No, I must be saved by Christ from first to last.

SIMEON: Suppose, then, that you were first turned by the grace of God, are you not in some way or other to keep yourself by your own power?

WESLEY: No.

SIMEON: Then are you to be upheld every moment and every hour by God, as much as an infant in its mother's arms?

WESLEY: Yes, altogether.

SIMEON: And is all your hope in the grace and mercy of God to preserve you unto his heavenly kingdom?

WESLEY: Yes, I have no hope but in Him.

Simeon was satisfied. He found no reason for combat. He put his figurative dagger back into its sheath.

Both these men were standing firmly on the grace platform.

Chapter Eight

Your Speech Betrays You

Those on the works platform betray their position by saying things like the following:

"I am doing my best." The trouble here is that your best is not good enough! All "the best" you have to offer is only filthy rags in God's sight.

"I'm not as bad as a lot of other people." That may be true, but you have fallen short of God's standard of perfection and you need to be saved.

"I'm trying to be a Christian. I am kind to my neighbors and I lead a good life." You can't become a Christian by trying. It is by trusting in the Lord Jesus.

"Isn't it enough that I am sincere?" A person can be sincere and yet sincerely wrong. Did you read about the father who came downstairs in the middle of the night, thinking that he had heard a robber? When he saw a movement in the living room, he fired his gun and killed his sweet, young daughter. He was sincere, but horribly mistaken.

"I have always been very religious." Sometimes the worst thing about a person is his religion. It hides from him his need of Christ.

Warren Wiersbe says,

Like most "religious" people today, Paul had enough morality to keep him out of trouble, but not enough righteousness to get him into heaven! It was not bad things that kept Paul away from Jesus—it was good things! He had to lose his 'religion' to find salvation.[1]

"I hope I'll get to heaven." It is not enough to hope; you must know. You must be certain. Perhaps your hope is wrong.

"My grandfather was a minister." This completely overlooks the fact that salvation is an intensely personal matter. Your grandfather's status doesn't save you. Grace doesn't run in the genes or by pedigree.

"You can't know until God brings out His scales." It will be too late then if you are depending on your works. You can know now if you receive the gift of God, namely, eternal life through the Lord Jesus.

"I think I have a good chance." You have no chance at all as long as you depend on yourself and not on the Saviour.

"It would be presumption for me to say I am saved." That would be true if salvation were by works. But when it is a free gift based on simple trust, there is no presumption. God says that those who repent and believe are saved. Is it presumption to believe that? No, it is presumption to *doubt* His Word. That is where the real presumption lies.

"I have to clean up my life first, don't I?" No, you don't. God invites you to come just as you are in all your sins. If you wait until you're better, you will never come. God is not looking for good people. He is looking for ungodly sinners whom He can save.

"I'm afraid I wouldn't be able to hold out." You will not have this fear once you realize that salvation is all of grace. You will be no more able to "hold out" than you are to save yourself in the first place. But the same wonderful Saviour who gives you salvation as a free gift is also able to "keep you from stumbling, and to present you faultless before the presence of His glory with exceeding joy."[2]

Notice the emphasis on self in all the foregoing quotes. Not one word about the Saviour. Such persons, who think that everything depends on what they themselves are or have done, will never know the sweetness of salvation by God's amazing grace.

Chapter Nine

WHAT'S WRONG WITH WORKS

It may seem from what we have said that we don't believe in works. That is a misunderstanding. When we say that we are not saved by works, we mean *meritorious* works, in other words, works that obligate God to save us. We mean works by which we seek to earn or deserve a place in heaven.

Actually, there is a sense in which even repentance and faith are works, but they are not *meritorious*. Repentance is turning around so that your face is toward God and your back toward sin. Faith is simply believing the Word of God, who cannot lie. Repentance is not something you boast about, and neither is faith. They are simply reasonable actions that everyone should take.

The first good work that a sinner can do is to believe on Christ. When the Jews asked Jesus, "What good work shall we do, that we may work the works of God?" Jesus answered, *"This is the work of God, that you believe in Him whom He has sent."*[1]

Until he does that, his good works are bad works in God's sight. The best he can offer is only filthy rags as far as the Lord is concerned.[2] But that all changes when a person is born again. From then on, anything he does in obedience to the Word of God is now a good work. Whatever he does as unto the Lord qualifies. Even the most common and menial tasks become good works when they are performed with a view to pleasing Him. We sometimes limit good works to deeds of mercy and charity, and to various forms of Christian service. But our daily duties at work and in the home count with God and will be rewarded at the Judgment Seat of Christ.

Good works are the *fruit* of salvation, not the *root:* the *result,* not the *cause.* The Bible is full of teaching that believers should do good works,[3] not *in order to* be saved but *because* they are saved. We are not saved *by* good works, but we are saved *unto* good works. They are the outcome and confirmation of salvation.

We should not separate what God has joined together. He has joined faith and salvation, works and reward. Just remember these two marriages and all will be well.

Chapter Ten

ANSWER ME THIS QUESTION

If you sin, you lose your salvation, don't you?

The question invariably arises, "When a believer sins, doesn't he lose his salvation?" Of course not. Consider the following:

Jesus said that no sheep of His would ever perish.[1] That should be enough to settle the matter. Salvation is a gift of grace. When God gives a gift, He never takes it back.[2] The same grace that saves also keeps.[3]

The gift of God is *eternal* life.[4] "Eternal" means *forever.* When a person is saved, he or she becomes a child of God by the new birth.[5] Once a birth takes place, it can never be changed or undone. It is forever. Relationship is an unbreakable chain.

Just as sure as one is justified, so sure is it that that person will one day be glorified.[6] The Holy Spirit indwells the believer forever,[7] not just until he sins. The Spirit is given to the believer as an earnest or pledge of heaven.[8] He is the guarantee of eventual glory. He also is a seal on the Christian, a proof of his ownership by the Lord, and of his security until he receives his glorified body in heaven.[9]

The Lord Jesus reconciled us to God when we were enemies. How much more will He keep us by His present ministry for us in heaven![10] He paid too high a price for us to ever let us go.

The believer will never be condemned.[11] God is his Father now, no longer his Judge. It was Christ who paid the penalty of the Christian's sins.[12] This means that the believer will never have to pay it. One payment settles it forever. The Lord Jesus finished the work.[13] You can't add to a finished work. And you don't have to. So nothing in the universe can separate a believer from God's love.[14]

It is true that there are some verses in the Bible that seem to say that a person can be saved, then lost again as a result of his or her sin. Many of these verses are speaking about nominal Christians rather than born-again believers. Other passages are dealing with service rather than salvation. And some describe apostates—those who once *professed* faith in Christ but who subsequently renounced Christ, indicating that they were never genuinely converted.

Yes, but suppose a believer does sin?

What then does happen when a believer sins? His fellowship with God is broken.[15] God is still his Father,[16] but *communion* with Him is interrupted. And his fellowship with fellow believers is broken.[17]

He loses the joy of his salvation.[18] He loses his power.[19] He loses any effective testimony;[20] his lips are sealed. He is still fit for heaven through the merits of Christ, but he is unfit for service on earth.

If the sin is of a public nature, he brings shame on the name of the Lord Jesus, and causes the Saviour's enemies to blaspheme.[21] He is living a lie. His actions cast doubt on the reality of his conversion.[22] It's a case of high talk, low walk. He talks cream but lives skim milk.

Sin blocks his prayer life.[23] His works will be burned up, but not he himself.[24] He may lose his health.[25] And he is in danger of making shipwreck of his life.[26] A single decision made by a backslider could put him on the shelf for the rest of his life as far as service for the Lord is concerned.

He may lose his *physical* life here on earth.[27] And he may lose rewards at the Judgment Seat of Christ.[28]

The situation is not hopeless, however. There is a way back to God. As soon as he confesses and forsakes his sin,[29] he receives forgiveness from God his Father. A   n   d 1 John 1:9 is emphatic on this point: *"If we confess our sins, He is faithful and just to forgive us our sins and to cleanse us from all unrighteousness."* The responsibility of the sinning saint is to confess, that is, to acknowledge his sins, calling them by their name, in the presence of God. He doesn't have to beg the Lord to forgive. He doesn't have to wail over them, although that might be very much in order. He simply confesses them from the heart.

God is faithful to forgive, because He promised that He would. He is just to forgive, because the substitutionary work of Christ provides a righteous way for Him to do so. And He not only forgives; He cleanses from all unrighteousness. The record is clear. The guilt is gone. The condemning voice of conscience is silenced.

The unsaved person receives judicial forgiveness of sins when he repents and believes on the Lord Jesus Christ. The Christian receives parental forgiveness of sins when he confesses.

One note of caution should be added. Although a

believer's sins are forgiven the moment he confesses them, the consequences of sin often remain. In that sense, he cannot sin and get away with it.

I know a man who was saved, then lost. How about that?

Several facts should be noted. First, there is a difference between those who only profess to be Christians and those who have been genuinely born again. There are nominal believers and genuine believers. If a person says he is saved, yet goes on continually in a life of sin, there is good reason for doubting his profession. When Christ comes in, He makes a difference in a life.

Then there are backsliders. They were truly converted but have wandered away from the Lord. Peter is an example. He really loved the Lord but fell into sin. Backsliders are either restored in this life through God's discipline or removed to heaven.

There is a another class known as apostates, of which Judas is an example. These people were never born again, but they pretend to be believers. Quite a few are actually baptized and received into a local church as members. But then they maliciously repudiate Christ and deny the Christian truth. It is impossible for these apostates to be converted.

In all these matters, we must not base our doctrine on

experience or emotion. The test is, "What does the Bible say?" The Bible says that a true believer is saved forever.

It's too easy. It isn't reasonable to think that salvation is a free gift. Don't you think your gospel is too cheap?

The biblical answer is that while it is free to us, it wasn't cheap for the Saviour. It cost Him everything. It's in the very nature of a gift to cost the giver but not the recipient. But people don't refuse birthday presents, wedding presents, or Christmas presents. Why refuse the greatest of all gifts?

Behind the "too cheap" objection lies human pride. People are incurably addicted to the notion that they can contribute something meritorious to purchase their own ticket to heaven. Because grace rules out that possibility, they don't like it. They reject it. What about you?

Chapter Eleven

GRACE MISUSED AND ABUSED

Like every other good thing, grace can be abused. Fire and water can be great blessings, but they can be used wrongly. People can twist the sovereignty of God to teach fatalism: what is going to be, is going to be; and there's nothing you can do about it. The doctrine of election is sometimes perverted to suggest that evangelizing is a waste of time and effort.

Sad to say, it is possible to use the grace of God as an excuse for careless living, for believers to use their freedom as a pretext for launching into all kinds of indulgence. This does not mean that the doctrine is faulty. It simply means that some people are desperate to justify ungodly behavior, and if they can do it by using Scripture, so much the better, or so they think.

It is true that believers are not under law but under grace.[1] But that does not mean that they have a right to be lawless. They are not under the law, with all the penalty and condemnation that is involved. But they are under law to Christ,[2] that is, they are bound to Christ by cords of love and constrained to do things that are pleasing in His sight. This relationship is well expressed in the verse:

> *Need I that a law should bind me*
> *Captive unto Thee?*
> *Captive is my heart, rejoicing*
> *Never to be free.*

It is true that when the Lord makes a person free, that person is free indeed.[3] But that does not mean freedom to sin. Liberty is not license. A pilot is free to explore the skies, but he'd better follow the assigned flight path if he wants to reach his destination safely. Paul taught the Galatians (and all believers), *"For you, brethren, have been called to liberty, only do not use liberty as an opportunity for the flesh... "*[4]

John MacArthur states it well:

Freedom from the law means freedom from sin's bondage and freedom from the law's penalty—not freedom from moral restraint. Grace does not mean we have permission to do as we please; it means we have the power to do what pleases God. The mere suggestion that God's grace gives us license to sin is self-contradictory, for the very purpose of grace is to free us from sin. How can we who are the recipients of grace continue in sin?[5]

Why do people use grace as a pretext for careless living? It may be that they are not truly saved. Think of the religious people who celebrate Mardi Gras. They engage in drunkenness and licentiousness right up to Tuesday night, planning to seek forgiveness on Ash Wednesday and hopefully to abstain from those sins during Lent.

It may be that others, though believers, are ignorant of the true doctrine of grace. It may be that they don't understand the truth of God's holiness. Or perhaps their idea of sin is too shallow. A person can be saved and yet be poorly taught.

It may be a willful ignorance on the part of some. They know what is required of them, but they are out of fellowship with the Lord. They are in a backslidden condition and are confident that God will overlook their "little" sins, their so-called "peccadillos."

Or again, it may be that they are apostates. Jude speaks of these unbelievers as *"ungodly men, who turn the grace of God into licentiousness and deny the only Lord God and our Lord Jesus Christ."*[6]

Chapter Twelve

HOW GOD PRODUCES HOLINESS

We have seen that salvation is by grace through faith and apart from works, but the question remains, "How is holiness achieved in the lives of those who are saved?" When a person becomes a Christian, there must be a change in his life. The question is, "What is the process that accomplishes this change?"

Actually there are only two conceivable ways. It is either by law or by grace. Just as these are the only two ways by which people hope to reach heaven, so they are the only ways in which they hope to produce holiness of life.

The most natural and humanistic way is to put people

under law. Give them a set of rules and regulations, of do's and don'ts. Tell them that they must keep these rules by their own strength. And since the law must have teeth in it, tell them that they will lose their salvation if they don't obey. This certainly seems to be the logical way to achieve sanctified lives. Otherwise people will go out and engage in all kinds of sinful behavior. That, at least, is the argument.

The trouble with law as a highway to holiness is that it doesn't work. People are no more able to live holy lives by their own strength than they were to save themselves in the first place. That is what Paul meant when he asked the Galatians, *"Having begun in the Spirit, are you now made perfect in the flesh?"* [1] The law tells people what to do, but it doesn't give the power to do it, and it condemns violators. Instead of leading to holiness, law has the opposite effect. Just as forbidden fruit is sweet, so when you tell a person not to do something, it awakens a desire in his fallen nature to do it. Law never produces holiness. All it can do is reveal sin and punish transgressors.

God's method is to produce holiness through grace. Let me explain. God says, in effect, "Look, I have saved you by My grace. Now, motivated by love to the Saviour, go out and live a life that is consistent with your profession."

Notice that under grace, love is the motive for holy living. And love is a stronger motive than fear. People will do out of love what they would never do through fear of punishment. Love for the Lord produces saintly living; fear never does.

Grace gives a believer a perfect standing before God on the basis of the work of Christ. Then it tells the believer to walk worthily of this standing. In other words, his state should increasingly correspond to his standing. His practice should become more and more like his position. He is called to be a son of God and he should walk like a member of the royal family. J. F. Strombeck says, "God first reminds of what He has done in grace; then on the basis of that, He appeals for a life in harmony with that which He has done."[2]

The child of God's position is what he is in Christ. Those words *"in Christ"* are the key to understanding his position before God. This is how God sees him because he has accepted the Lord Jesus as his Saviour. His practice is what he is in everyday life.

Unfortunately, a Christian's state will never *perfectly* correspond to his standing in this life. But it should be increasingly moving in that direction. When he is glorified with Christ in heaven, his practice will be perfect, but it is more glorifying to God if great progress is made down here.

Some of the adjectives that describe position are: regenerated, forgiven, reconciled, redeemed, accepted, complete, perfected, justified, sanctified, and glorified.

Some of the verbs that describe practice are: be, do, walk, present, offer, give, reckon, stand, let, put away, put on, should, ought, and yield.

God's method, then, is to give the believer a perfect position before Him, then teach him to walk in harmony with it. This is the very opposite of law. The latter says, "If you reach a certain state, you will earn your standing." Impossible, of course! It can't be done. Grace says, "I give you the position as a free gift; now walk worthily of it." This can be done by the power of the indwelling Holy Spirit.

Perhaps you have heard of the widower who hired a housekeeper to care for his children and his house. He posted a set of rules on the refrigerator door, and let her know quite clearly that these were her responsibilities.

Then the plot thickened. He fell in love with the charming lady, and as soon as they were married, he removed the rules from the fridge. She kept doing the work—and more—and better—but she was doing it now out of love, and not out of fear of losing her job.

When properly understood, grace is the strongest possible motive for holy living. Think of it this way! The Lord Jesus died to put away the sins of believers by the sacrifice of Himself. Do they now want to go on in that which caused His death? He has proved Himself to be His people's dearest Friend. Should they not make it their aim to be well-pleasing to Him in all that they do and say?

When He died, He died as their representative. When He died, they died. Positionally, they are dead to sin. In practice, they should reckon themselves as being dead to sin. Paul argues the point in Romans 6. He asks, *"Shall we continue in sin that grace may abound?"*[3] Then he answers indignantly, *"Certainly not! How shall we who died to sin live any longer in it?"*[4] Before a person is saved by grace, he is a slave of sin. Now he is a servant of righteousness. He should yield himself to this holy slavery.

Someone put it this way: Reason back from the greatness of the Sacrifice to the greatness of the sin; then determine to be done with sin forever.

John Bunyan expressed it even more strongly:

Sin is the dare of God's justice, the rape of His mercy, the jeer of His patience, the slight of His power, and the contempt of His love.

The bridge separating God's people from sin was purchased at too great a price for them to walk back over it.

What is a worthy walk?

The question now is, "How can I know what a worthy walk is?" The answer is given in the practical instructions that are found in God's Word. The New Testament has hundreds of such commandments, but here we must quickly add a word of explanation. The commands found there are not given as law with penalty attached. Rather they are instructions in righteousness that answer the question, "What kind of behavior is suitable for a person who has been saved by grace?" Here are some examples, found in a single passage of Scripture:[5]

> *"Putting away lying, each one speak truth with his neighbor..."* *"Be angry, and do not sin." "Let him who stole steal no longer, but rather let him labor, working with his hands what is good, that he may have something to give to him who has need." "Let no corrupt communication proceed out of your mouth." "Do not grieve the Holy Spirit of God." "Let all bitterness, wrath, anger, clamor, and evil speaking be put away from you, with all malice." "And be kind to one another, tender-hearted, forgiving one another, just as God in Christ also forgave you."*

So we see that the same grace that has brought salvation also teaches that, *"denying ungodliness and worldly lusts, we should live soberly, righteously, and godly in the present age."*[6]

Strombeck points out that

> ...the present low level of Christian conduct is largely due to incomplete teaching of grace. All misconceptions on the part of many, that an over-emphasis on grace is license to sin, would quickly be removed if grace were preached and understood in its fullness.[7]

My Hiding Place

Hail, sovereign love, which first began
The scheme to rescue fallen man!
Hail, matchless, free, eternal grace,
Which gave my soul a Hiding Place.

Against the God who built the sky
I fought with hands uplifted high—
Despised the mention of His grace,
Too proud to seek a Hiding Place.

Enwrapt in thick Egyptian night,
And fond of darkness more than light,
Madly I ran the sinful race,
Secure—without a Hiding Place.

But thus the eternal counsel ran:
Almighty love, arrest that man!
I felt the arrows of distress,
And found I had no Hiding Place.

Indignant Justice stood in view:
To Sinai's fiery mount I flew;
But Justice cried with frowning face,
This mountain is no Hiding Place!

NOW *THAT* IS AMAZING GRACE!

Ere long a heavenly voice I heard,
And mercy's angel soon appeared:
He led me, with a beaming face,
To Jesus as a hiding place.

On Him almighty vengeance fell,
Which must have sunk a world to hell!
He bore it for a sinful race,
And thus became their Hiding Place.

Should sevenfold storms of thunder roll,
And shake this globe from pole to pole,
No thunderbolt shall daunt my face,
For Jesus is my Hiding Place.

A few more setting suns at most
Shall land me on fair Canaan's coast,
Where I shall sing the song of grace,
And see my glorious Hiding Place.

Major John André was carrying these verses when he was captured on September 23, 1780. It is not known whether he was the one who wrote them.

Chapter Thirteen

IT'S GRACE ALL THE WAY

The Christian life is grace from beginning to end. The God of all grace never ceases to shower His favor on those who love Him. At times, His mercy may be veiled from view, but looking back, it is clear that He had never forgotten to be kind.

Believers see divine grace in the miracle of their preservation. Considering all the diseases in circulation, and the innumerable possibilities of accidents, and the hazards of travel, and the peril of violent men, it is nothing short of a marvel that life goes on at all.

Think of the Lord's grace in guidance. So many people to direct, and yet He does it with infinite care and consummate skill, so that each one can say:

> *With mercy and with judgment*
> *My web of time He wove.*

Each one can sing: "My Jesus has done all things well." At times, the route is through a trackless desert; at other times it is like a minefield. Yet in all life's chapters, He leads "with sweet, unwearied care the flock for which He bled."

And then there is His grace in provision. The generous God provides every need of His loved ones according to His inexhaustible riches in glory by Christ Jesus. He feeds them with the finest of wheat, and honey from the rock,[1] and gives them their food in due season.

His providence manifests itself also in His absolute control of circumstances and in His timing and sequence of events. In His grace, He guarantees that nothing happens by chance. Rather He works all things together for good to those who love Him. Because His children are the apple of His eye, He promises that no weapon formed against them will prosper, and every tongue that rises against them shall be condemned.[2] He overrules the wickedness of the ungodly for His glory and the benefit of His people.

Never does the Lord's grace shine with

greater splendor than in His forgiveness. No one can measure its dimensions. Think of the case of the king called David. First he committed adultery with Bathsheba while her husband, Uriah, was off at war. When David summoned this faithful lieutenant back from battle, the king tried to arrange circumstances so that Uriah would appear to be the father of the expected baby. Failing in this, David devised the low-down stratagem of sending Uriah where he would be most exposed to enemy fire, and where his death was assured. The king's immorality and treachery were contemptible and unworthy of such a monarch. Yet as soon as he repented, he heard the emancipating words, *"The Lord...has put away your sin."* It is this supernatural kind of forgiveness that led Samuel Davies to write:

> *Great God of wonders! all Thy ways*
> *Display Thine attributes divine;*
> *But the bright glories of Thy grace*
> *Above Thine other wonders shine:*
> *Who is a pardoning God like Thee?*
> *Or who has grace so rich and free?*
>
> *Such deep transgressions to forgive!*
> *Such guilty, daring worms to spare!*
> *This is Thy grand prerogative*
> *And in this honor none shall share:*
> *Who is a pardoning God like Thee?*
> *Or who has grace so rich and free?*

Our God gives sustaining grace to His people in every time of need. Facing surgery, Christians can know a peace that is completely outside their own resources. In sickness, they can experience a strength that can only come from everlasting arms that are underneath. Martyrs receive an other-worldly courage to endure the rifle and fire. And God gives dying grace to His own when their work on earth is done—but they don't get the grace till then.

The greatest display of grace was when He who was rich beyond calculation became poor beyond measure that unworthy sinners might be enriched beyond imagination.

It was unspeakable grace that prayed from Calvary, *"Father, forgive them, for they do not know what they do."* [3]

It was divine grace that moved God to send His Holy Spirit back to the very city where His incarnate Son had been murdered a short time before.

Because God is the dispenser of matchless grace, the Psalmist could say with classic understatement that the Lord's thoughts toward His own are more numerous than the sands of the sea, [4] and His faithfulness reaches to the clouds. [5] How glad believers can be that He has not dealt with them according to their sins, nor punished them according to their iniquities. [6] *"His compassions fail not.*

They are new every morning."[7]

It is grace without limit from natural life to spiritual life to eternal life. And it will be the theme of praise forever and ever.

Chapter Fourteen

GRACE IN REVIEW

Now let us review the highlights in our contemplation of the grandeur of God's grace.

The question we address first is this: In devising a plan of salvation, how can God, who is holy and just, pardon sinners and still be just in doing so.

The answer lies in the single word *substitution*. God sent His unique Son, the Lord Jesus Christ, to die as a substitute for sinners on Calvary's cross. He paid the penalty in full and now gives everlasting life as a free gift to all who believe on Him.

This is pure grace—God's unmerited favor to those

who deserve the very opposite. In order to appreciate that grace, we must realize who Jesus is; what He did; the ones for whom He did it; and the blessings that flow to those who receive Him by faith.

There is only one other religion in the world. It is called another gospel, but it is not good news at all. It teaches that people reach heaven by their own goodness or attainments. It is the most popular religion because it caters to human pride. In spite of its grandiose claims, it offers neither assurance of salvation, present security, nor eternal life. It leads to hell at last.

People who are saved by grace give all the honor to the Lord Jesus. Those who believe in salvation by works claim the glory for themselves, or at least part of it. That's how you can tell on what a person is basing his hopes for heaven.

When we say that salvation is not by good works, that does not mean that we are opposed to good works. We are not! What we want to emphasize is that works are not the root of salvation; they are the fruit. We are not saved *by* good works; we are saved *unto* them. They are not the procuring cause, but the result, not the origin but the outcome.

The question naturally arises, "If a person sins after he is saved, does he lose his salvation?" The consistent testimony of Scripture and the true nature of grace require an emphatic *No* for an answer. Sin breaks fellowship but not relationship. Fellowship is a tender thread, whereas relationship is an unbreakable chain. As soon as a believer confesses his sin, he is forgiven, and fellowship with the Lord is restored.

Not everyone who *professes* to be a Christian is actually saved. If sin is the dominating power in someone's life, if he or she lives in sin, there is good reason to doubt that person's conversion. He may be a professor but not a possessor. When Christ comes into a life, He makes a difference.

To those who object that the gospel of grace is too cheap, it should be enough to remind them that the one who presents a gift is the one who pays, not the one who receives it. It is in the very nature of a gift that it costs the donor, not the recipient. God, as Donor, paid an enormous price to give eternal life as a free gift.

Like all good things, grace can be abused. People can use it as an excuse for indulgence and evil. But in all such cases, the problem lies with the individual, not with the doctrine of grace.

Grace, not law, is the strongest possible motive for holy living. The law demands performance and threatens punishment for failure. Grace tells what Christ has done and urges a corresponding life of holiness. The God of grace puts the believer in a position of perfect favor before

Him, then calls for a life that is in harmony with that position. The detailed instructions of the New Testament clearly describe what is a worthy walk.

The life of the child of God is a display of divine grace from beginning to end. It is a revelation of God, who owes man nothing, showering him with unimaginable blessings. It is the story of the Lord giving His best to those who deserve nothing but His judgment.

God is still searching for men and women to whom He can show His amazing grace. Undeterred by centuries of human indifference, reluctance, and refusal, the God of all grace is still sending out the good news, seeking the sheep that are lost. He is looking for those who will admit that they are guilty, who will stop trying to save themselves, and who will believe on Jesus as Lord and Saviour. It's just as simple as that!

And remember this! Wherever God finds a spark of *genuine faith* in the Lord Jesus, He will reckon that person to be righteous. As H. A. Ironside said,

> God thinks so much of the Person and work of His Son that He will have everyone in heaven who will give Him the least possible excuse for getting him there. What matchless grace.[1]

The last chapter has not been written. Throughout eternity, God will be revealing the exceeding riches of His grace in His kindness toward us in Christ Jesus.[2] It will be an everlasting unfolding of His wonderful plan of salvation, of all it meant to Him to send His Son to this jungle of sin to seek and to save those who were lost—and of all the blessings that have come to us through that wonderful work at Calvary!

The Bible ends on a grace note, and so will we: *"The grace of our Lord Jesus Christ be with you all. Amen."*

ENDNOTES

INTRODUCTION
  1. Words by John Newton (1725-1807)

CHAPTER TWO:
  1. 1 Timothy 2:5
  2. John 1:1
  3. 2 Corinthians 5:21; 1 Peter 2:22; 1 John 3:5
  4. 1 John 1:7
  5. Psalm 40:8; Hebrews 12:2
  6. Isaiah 53:4-6
  7. John 1:29
  8. Galatians 2:20
  9. 1 Peter 2:24
  10. 1 John 2:2
  11. John 3:16
  12. 1 John 2:2
  13. Romans 3:23
  14. Matthew 11:28
  15. Revelation 22:17

16. John 3:36
17. Psalm 85:10
18. *The Applause of Heaven,* Dallas, TX: Word Publishing, 1990, pp. 175-176
19. John F. MacArthur, Jr., *Faith Works,* Dallas, TX: Word Publishing, 1993, p. 99
20. Quoted in *Baptist Biblical Heritage,* Apr. 94, p. 1

CHAPTER THREE:

1. Hebrews 4:10
2. Jn. 1:12; 3:15-16, 36; 5:24; 6:40, 47; 7:37-38; 11:25-26; 20:31; Acts 16:31; Rom. 10:9; Gal. 3:22-26; Eph. 2:8; 1 Jn. 5:10-13

CHAPTER FOUR:

1. Ephesians 2:8-9
2. Psalm 40:1-3
3. *Surprised by Joy* (New York, NY: Harcourt Brace Jovanovich, Publishers, 1984), p. 229
4. Matthew 20:1-16
5. 1 Thessalonians 4:1. Note also such expressions of grace as "I beseech you" (Romans 12:1)

CHAPTER FIVE:

1. Isaiah 40:12
2. Quoted in *Baptist Biblical Heritage,* Apr. 94, p. 1
3. Jeremiah 17:9
4. Romans 3:23
5. Ephesians 2:2-3, 12
6. Our Daily Bread, Apr. 20, 1994
7. Quoted in *The Power of Story,* Leighton Ford, Colorado Springs, CO: Navpress, 1994, p. 112
8. *The Heart of the Gospel,* Wheaton, IL: Crossway, 1991, pp. 165-166
9. Romans 6:23
10. John 10:10

11. Colossians 1:27
12. Ephesians 1:7
13. Colossians 2:14
14. 1 Peter 1:18
15. Ephesians 2:5
16. Ephesians 1:6
17. Colossians 2:10
18. John 17:23
19. Romans 5:1
20. Hebrews 10:10
21. Heb. 4:14-16; Rom. 8:34; 1 Jn. 2:1; Jn. 14:16
22. John 14:16-17
23. 1 Corinthians 12:13
24. Ephesians 1:13
25. Ephesians 1:14
26. 1 John 2:27
27. Ephesians 2:18
28. Hebrews 10:19
29. Philippians 3:20
30. John 1:12
31. Galatians 4:6
32. Romans 8:17
33. 1 Peter 2:5, 9
34. Romans 8:37
35. 1 John 3:2
36. Ephesians 1:3
37. C.H. Spurgeon, *Sermons on the Book of Daniel,* Grand Rapids, MI: Zondervan, 1966, p. 54
38. *Persuasion,* London: MacDonald and Jane's, 1974, p. 273
39. Romans 5:20b

CHAPTER SIX:

1.Proverbs 14:12
2.Romans 11:6
3. Luke 18:18

4. Romans 3:20, 28; 4:5; Galatians 2:16; 3:10-11; Ephesians 2:9;
2 Timothy 1:9; Titus 3:5
5. Romans 3:20, 28; 4:1-12; Galatians 2:16-17; 3:10-14; Eph. 2:8-
9; 2 Timothy 1:9; Titus 3:5
6. Romans 4:16
7. Galatians 4:28-31

CHAPTER SEVEN:
1. Ruth 2:10
2. 2 Samuel 7:18
3. 2 Samuel 9:8
4. Ephesians 3:8-9
5. From *Victorious Christians You Should Know,* Warren W.
Wiersbe (Grand Rapids, MI: Baker, 1984), pp. 63-64
6. Arminians emphasize man's free will in salvation, whereas
Calvinists emphasize God's sovereignty and election. The conversation shows that if the terms of salvation are used according to
their biblical usage, the two views are not necessarily mutually
exclusive.

CHAPTER EIGHT:
1. *The Bible Exposition Commentary,* Vol. 2, Wheaton, IL: Victor
Books, 1989, p. 84
2. Jude 24

CHAPTER NINE:
1. John 6:29
2. Isaiah 64:6
3. John 12:26; 1 Corinthians 3:8; Ephesians 2:10; 6:8; Titus 3:8;
Hebrews 6:10; Revelation 22:12

CHAPTER TEN:
1. John 10:27-28
2. Romans 11:29
3. 1 Peter 1:5; Jude 1c, 24

4. Romans 6:23
5. John 1:12
6. Romans 8:30
7. John 14:16
8. 2 Corinthians 1:22; 5:5; Ephesians 1:14
9. 2 Corinthians 1:22; Ephesians 1:13; 4:30
10. Romans 5:10
11. John 5:24
12. 1 Corinthians 15:3
13. John 19:30
14. Romans 8:38-39
15. 1 John 1:6
16. 1 John 2:1b
17. 1 John 1:7
18. Psalm 51:12
19. Psalm 32:4
20. Genesis 19:14b
21. 2 Samuel 12:14
22. 2 Timothy 2:19b
23. Psalm 66:18
24. 1 Corinthians 3:15
25. 1 Corinthians 11:30a
26. 1 Corinthians 9:27
27. 1 Corinthians 11:30b
28. 1 Corinthians 3:15b
29. Proverbs 28:13

CHAPTER ELEVEN:

1. Romans 6:14
2. 1 Corinthians 9:21
3. John 8:36
4. Galatians 5:13
5. John F. MacArthur, Jr., *Faith Works,* Dallas, TX: Word Publishing, 1993, p. 120
6. Jude 4

CHAPTER TWELVE:

1. Galatians 3:3
2. J. F. Strombeck, *Disciplined by Grace,* Moline, IL: Grace and Truth, 1946, p. 102
3. Romans 6:1
4. Romans 6:2
5. Ephesians 4:25-32
6. Titus 2:12
7. J. F. Strombeck, *Disciplined By Grace,* p. 20

CHAPTER THIRTEEN:

1. Psalm 81:16
2. Isaiah 54:17
3. Luke 23:34
4. Psalm 139:17-18
5. Psalm 36:5
6. Psalm 103:10
7. Lamentations 3:22-23

CHAPTER FOURTEEN:

1. H. A. Ironside, *The Levitical Offerings,* Neptune, NJ: Loizeaux, 1982, p. 64
2. Ephesians 2:7

CPSIA information can be obtained
at www.ICGtesting.com
Printed in the USA
FSOW02n0430111016
25875FS

9 781882 701216